Jain Alphabet Book

(JAINA Education Series 103 - Level 1)

Nishi
Shah

Compiled by
JAINA Education Committee
Pravin K. Shah, Chairperson
Federation of Jain Associations in North America

Jain Alphabet Book

(JAINA Education Series 103 - Level 1)

Third Edition (revised): April 2003

ISBN: 1-59406-002-9

This book has no copyright

Please use the religious material respectfully

Published and Distributed by :
JAINA Education Committee
Pravin K. Shah, Chairperson
Federation of Jain Associations in North America
509 Carriage Woods Circle
Raleigh, NC 27607-3969 USA
Telephone and Fax - 919-859-4994

Email - education@jaina.org
Websites – www.jaina.org

Please provide us your comments and suggestions. Support JAINA Education activities. Your contribution is tax deductible in USA. Use the above address for communication.

Printed in Korea
by Oriental Art Press

Dedicated

to

Young Jains of America (YJA)
(www.yja.org)

Young Jain Professionals (YJP) and
(www.yjponline.org)

Jain Päthashälä Teachers of North America
(www.jaina.org)

for their continued effort and commitment in promoting religious awareness, nonviolence, reverence for all life forms, protection of the environment, and a spirit of compassionate interdependence with nature and all living beings. As importantly, for their commitment to the practice of Jainism, consistent with our principles, including vegetarianism and an alcohol/drug free lifestyle.

Our great appreciation to all the Päthashälä Teachers for their effort in instilling the basic values of Jainism and promoting the principles of non-violence and compassion to all youth and adults.

Special thanks to all Jain Vegan and alcohol/drug-free youth and adults for inspiring us to see the true connection between our beliefs and our choices.

A vegan and alcohol/drug-free lifestyle stems from a desire to minimize harm to all animals as well as to our own bodies, minds, and souls. As a result, one avoids the use of all animal products such as milk, cheese, butter, ghee, ice cream, silk, wool, pearls, leather, meat, fish, chicken, eggs and refrains from all types of addictive substances such as alcohol and drugs.

Acknowledgements

The project of compiling, revising, and editing of the existing JAINA Education series books was accomplished by a dedicated group of Päthashälä teachers, educators, and individuals of North America, India and other parts of the world. The devoted contribution of all these supporters is evident on every page of this series, and is gratefully acknowledged.

We would like to extend special thanks to the following people who contributed in the revision and publication of JAINA Education series Books.

For Revising and Editing the Contents:

Pradip & Darshana Shah	– Chicago IL
Mukesh Doshi	– Chicago IL
Parul Shah	– Raleigh NC
Harendra Shah	– Freemont CA
Sudhir & Anita Shah	– Woodbridge CT
Jadavji Kenia	– Dallas TX
Neha & Rakesh Jain	– Columbus OH
Alap Shah	– Chicago IL
Shanti Mohnot	– Pittsburgh PA
Samuel Wallace	– Raleigh NC
Shweta Shah	– Austin TX

For Guidance:

Muni Shri Nandighosh-Vijayji M.S.
Muni Shri Ajayasagarji M.S.

For Cover Design:

Narendra Velani	– Chicago IL

For Layout:

Michelle Rudolph	– Raleigh NC
Hemant Parikh	– Ahmedabad India

For Graphics, Software, Website, Articles, and Other Support:

Indrajit Shah	– Chicago IL
Ashish Modi	– Raleigh NC
Lalit Shah	– Ahmedabad India
Rajesh Khajuria	– Vadodara India
Kusumben Shah	– Ahmedabad India

For Publishing, Printing, Layout, and Distribution Support:

Rajendra Mehta	– Orlando FL
Kusumben Shah	– Ahmedabad India
Virendra Shah	– Los Angeles CA

Supporters of JAINA Education Activity:

The estimated cost of printing all of the education books will be approximately $50,000 to $60,000. We have received enthusiastic support in terms of advance payment from various Jain organizations and contributions from various individuals as follows:

The Support Organizations:

Jain Center of Chicago IL	$5,000.00
Jain Center of Northern California CA	$5,000.00
Jain Center of New York NY	$3,000.00
Jain Society of Houston TX	$3,000.00
Jain Center So. California - Los Angeles	$3,000.00
Jain Society Detroit	$3,000.00
Jain Center of Toronto	$1,500.00
Jain Society of Metro Washington DC	$1,000.00
Jain Society of Dallas TX	$1,000.00
Jain Center of Boston	$1,000.00
Jain Society of Pittsburgh PA	$1,000.00
Jain Society of Greater Cleveland OH	$1,000.00
Jain Study Center NC - Raleigh	$500.00
Jain Center of Minnesota	$500.00
Jain Center of Connecticut	$500.00
Jain Center of Louisiana	$500.00
Tulsa Jain Sangh - Tulsa OK	$500.00
Jain Society of San Diego - CA	$500.00
Jain Society of South Louisiana	$400.00
Jain Society of Las Vegas	$200.00

The Benefactors:

Riddhi Desai - Houston TX
Mahendra & Saroj Shah - Detroit MI
Suketu and Hetal Khandhar - Los Angeles CA
Hemen and Bela Gandhi - Olathe KS
Santosh and Bhakti Shah - Gretna LA
Andrea Argenton - Italy
Anonymous - California
Anonymous - Ohio

JAINA Education Series Books
(3ᴿᴰ Edition Revised)

Book Number	Level	Age	Publication Date	Title
JES-101	One	5-9	08-15-03	Jain Activity Book (Old Coloring book and Dot to Dot Book combined)
JES-102	One	5-9	Merged	Jain Dot to Dot Book merged in JES-101
JES-103	One	5-9	08-31-03	Jain Alphabets
JES-104	One	5-9	09-15-03	Jain Moral Skits
JES-201	Two	10-12	09-30-03	Jain Sutras and Stavans *
JES-202	Two	10-12	09-30-03	Jain Story Book
JES-203	Two	10-12	09-30-03	First Steps to Jainism I
JES-204	Two	10-12	09-30-03	First Steps to Jainism II
JES-301	Three	13-15	12-31-03	First Steps to Jainism III
JES-302	Three	13-15	03-15-03	Jain Philosophy and Practice I
JES-401	Four	16 up	09-30-03	Jain Philosophy and Practice II
JES-CD	All	All	08-01-02	JAINA Education CD
JES-900 Series	——	——		Reference Books

*Note – JES-201 and JES-301 books are new editions

PREFACE

Jai Jinendra

Non-violence (Ahimsä) is the backbone and focal point of Jain philosophy. Non-violence, non-absolutistic (Anekäntaväd) viewpoint, and non-possession / non-attachment (Aparigraha) are fundamental principles of Jainism. Non-violence strengthens the proper conduct of every individual, non-absolutistic viewpoints strengthens right thinking of every individual, and non-possession strengthen the interdependence of all existence and provides harmony in society. If we observe these three principles in their true spirit, peace and harmony can certainly be attained within us as well as in the world.

Although not fully introduced to the western world, Jainism is India's oldest living religion. The basic principles of Jainism are scientific and the 'truths' presented in our scriptures are universal, however, their interpretations and applications have to be done in the context of time and space in which we find ourselves.

In English-speaking countries where many Jains have settled permanently such as the USA, Canada, the UK, and Africa, children do not have access to Jain educational materials. In an attempt to make Jain principles known globally, the educational materials must be widely made available in English. It is also necessary to publish Jain literature and educational material in a variety of media (i.e. books, videos, cassettes, CDs, DVDs, and web deployment) for the English-speaking people interested in Jain philosophy, religion, and scriptures.

The JAINA Education Committee is pleased to present a set of JAINA Education books (revised 3rd edition) for all ages of students interested in learning Jainism. These books are grouped into four age levels: level 1 for elementary, level 2 for middle school, level 3 for high school, and level 4 for college students. The entire list of JAINA Education Series Books is listed in this section.

In 1995 and 1997, the first two editions of these books were published by the committee under the leadership of Dr. Premchand Gada of Lubbock, Texas. It took several years of his dedicated hard work to compile and publish this series of books. The Jain community of North America has greatly benefited from this effort.

Under a new JAINA Education committee, this 3rd edition series has gone through major revisions incorporating suggestions received from various Päthashälä teachers, educators, and students from different centers. The new committee members are Jain Päthashälä teachers of various centers and they have spent countless hours in the preparation of this material. Great care has been taken to present the material in a non-sectarian way and incorporated the uniqueness of every Jain sect. Most of the books have been rewritten with the addition of many new topics. Significant effort has been made to maintain consistency in the spellings of Jain words. Many youth have helped us in improving the English grammar in these books. The names of people who helped us in the preparation of this series are also listed in this section.

Jain scriptures are written using Devanägari characters. To correctly pronounce these characters in English, it is necessary to put various diacritical marks on some English vowels and consonants. However, most internet browsers and word processors do not display and print all transliterated characters. The main objective of these books is to teach principles of Jainism to Jain youth and lay people who do not have the knowledge of this transliteration convention. As a result a simplified diacritical mark scheme has been adopted for this series. The transliteration used here is neither authentic nor totally consistent. While it will serve the purpose of learning Jain principles, this book should not be used for learning correct pronunciations.

The estimated cost of preparation and reprinting this education series will be $60,000. We have received great enthusiastic support in terms of advance payment from various Jain organizations and contributions from various individuals. Please generously support JAINA education activity. We distribute the religious books on a cost basis. The names of financial supporters are listed in this section.

The Jain Alphabet Book (JES 103 - Level 1) for young children was recompiled using the 2nd edition book. Both the contents and the grammar were improved by adults and youth volunteers. Also the members may have used other sources, and we are grateful to the authors and publishers for being able to use their work liberally.

Please remember that the committee members are Jain Päthashälä teachers and are not Jain scholars. Hence, you may find some errors in the presentation. Certain items may be applicable to one Jain sect and not applicable to other sects of Jainism. Please pardon us for any mistakes, oversights, understatements, or overstatements in the material. We request you to use and review the material objectively and provide suggestions to enable us to easily incorporate them in future revisions.

In line with Jain Philosophy, the JAINA education series is not copyrighted. However, if you need to copy and distribute any of the materials, please do it respectfully and on a cost basis. Please note that most of these books and other materials are available on JAINA Education CD and from the JAINA website - *www.jaina.org*.

A lot of minds and blessings, both directly and indirectly, have touched this noble project. We sincerely appreciate and thank every person and every organization that made this project successful. As always, if you have any comments and suggestions for improvement, please feel free to contact us.

If we have mentioned anything against the teachings of the Tirthankars, we ask for forgiveness.

Michchhämi Dukkadam.

Pravin K. Shah, Chairperson
JAINA Education Committee
education@jaina.org
August 1, 2003

Pronunciation Guide and a
Disclaimer note on Transliteration

Jain scriptures are written using Devanägari characters. To correctly pronounce these characters in English, it is necessary to put various diacritical marks on some English vowels and consonants. Scholars usually follow a standard transliteration scheme adopted by the International Congress of Orientalists at Athens, Greece in 1912.

However, most Internet browsers and word processors may not display and print all transliterated characters. The main objective of these Jain education series has been to teach Jainism concepts to Jain youth and lay people who do not have the knowledge of this transliteration convention. As a result, a following simplified scheme has been adopted for this series.

Only one diacritical mark, two dots over the letter "ä" (aa) or "Ä" (AA) is used to indicate a long vowel sound of letter "ä" associated with certain words.

The transliteration used here is neither authentic nor totally consistent. Therefore, while it will serve the purpose of learning Jain concepts, this book should not be used for learning correct pronunciations.

The pronunciation guide is as listed below. The bold letter in each Sanskrut word should be pronounced similarly to the bold letter in each English word. Please do not pronounce ä (aa) if the letter "a" but not "ä" appears at the end of word such as Karma or Jina.

English vowel	English word	Sanskrut or Präkrut word
A	ago	Karma
Ä	fär	Ätmä
I	police	Jina
U	rule	guru
E	red	Deva
O	go	ogho

Note - The Jain Sutra book (JES 201) will have all diacritical marks in the transliteration portion of the original Sutras.

Table of Contents

Preface   vii

Mangalächaran   xii

A is for Ahimsä   1

B is for Bowing Down (Vandan)   3

C is for Charity   5

D is for Discipline   7

E is for Evening Prayer and Pratikraman   9

F is for Forgiveness   11

G is for Guru (Sädhu and Sädhvi)   13

H is for Help   17

I is for Indrabhuti Gautam (Gautam Swämi)   19

J is for Jai-Jinendra   23

K is for Karma   25

L is for Leshyä   27

M is for Mahävir   31

N is for Navakär Mantra   35

O is for Om   39

P is for Päthashälä   41

Q is for Queen Trishalä   43

R is for Rosary   45

S is for Soul (Ätmä)   47

T is for Temple   49

U is for Upäshray   51

V is for Vow   53

W is for Worship   55

X is for Xylography   57

Y is for Yoga   59

Z is for Zälar   61

Color Science of Navakär Mantra   63

Mangalächaran

नवकारमंत्र   *navakära mantra*

नमो अरिहंताणं ।	namo arihantänarm ।
नमो सिद्धाणं ।	namo siddhänam ।
नमो आयरियाणं ।	namo äyariyänam ।
नमो उवज्झायाणं ।	namo uvajjhäyänam ।
नमो लोए सव्वसाहूणं ।	namo loe savvasähünam ।
एसो पंच नमुक्कारो ।	eso pancha namukkäro ।
सव्वपावप्पणासणो ।	savvapävappanäsano ।
मंगलाणं च सव्वेसिं	mangalänam cha savvesim
पढमं हवई मंगलं ॥	padhamam havai mangalam ॥

I bow to Arihantas (Tirthankars), the perfected souls, who have reached enlightenment by overcoming their inner weaknesses, who have attained infinite knowledge, perception, bliss, and power and have shown the path, which brings an end to the cycle of birth, life, death and suffering.

I bow to Siddhas, the liberated souls, who have attained the state of perfection and immortality by eradicating all karma.

I bow to Ächäryas, who are the head of Jain congregation, and who preach the principles of religion and show the path of liberation, which is the unity of Right Faith, Right Knowledge, and Right Conduct.

I bow to Upädhyäys who are the ascetic teachers. They explain Jain scriptures and show us the importance of a spiritual life over a material life.

I bow to all Sädhus and Sädhvis who strictly follow the five great vows of conduct and inspire us to live a simple life.

To these five types of great souls I offer my praise.

Such praise will help diminish my negative vibrations and sins.

Offering this praise is most auspicious of all benedictions.

चत्तारि मंगलं

chattäri mangalam

चत्तारि मंगलं, अरिहंता मंगलं,
सिद्धा मंगलं, साहू मंगलं,
केवलिपण्णत्तो धम्मो मंगलं ।

chattäri mangalam, arihantä mangalam,
siddhä mangalam, sähü mangalam,
kevalipannatto dhammo mangalam I

चत्तारि लोगुत्तमा, अरिहंता लोगुत्तमा,
सिद्धा लोगुत्तमा, साहू लोगुत्तमा,
केवलिपण्णत्तो धम्मो लोगुत्तमो ।

chattäri loguttamä, arihantä loguttamä,
siddhä loguttamä, sähü loguttamä,
kevalipannatto dhammo loguttamo I

चत्तारि शरणं पवज्जामि, अरिहंते शरणं
पवज्जामि,
सिद्धे शरणं पवज्जामि, साहू शरणं
पवज्जामि,
केवलि पण्णत्तं धम्मं शरणं पवज्जामि ॥

chattäri sharanam pavajjämi, arihante
sharanam pavajjämi,
siddhe sharanam pavajjämi, sähü
sharanam pavajjämi,
kevalipannattam dhammam sharanam
pavajjämi II

There are four auspicious entities in the universe.
The Arihantas are auspicious.
The Siddhas are auspicious.
The Sädhus are auspicious.
The religion explained by the omniscient is auspicious.

There are four supreme entities in the universe.
The Arihantas are supreme.
The Siddhas are supreme.
The Sädhus are supreme.
The religion explained by the omniscient is supreme.

I take refuge in the four entities of the universe.
I take refuge in the Arihantas.
I take refuge in the Siddhas.
I take refuge in the Sädhus.
I take refuge in the religion explained by the omniscient.

दर्शनं देवदेवस्य, दर्शनं पापनाशनम् ।
दर्शन स्वर्गसोपानं, दर्शनं मोक्षसाधनम् ॥

darshanam devadevasya darshanam päpanäshanam
darshanam svargasopänam darshanam mokshasädhanam II

The sight of the idol of the Lord, the God of all heavenly gods, is the destroyer of all sins. It is a step towards the heavens, and is a means to the liberation of the soul.

मंगलं भगवान वीरो, मंगलं गौतम प्रभु ।
मंगलं स्थूलिभद्राद्या, जैन धर्मोस्तु मंगलं ॥

mangalam bhagaväna viro, mangalam gautama prabhu I
mangalam sthülibhadrädyä, jaina dharmostu mangalam II

Bhagawän Mahävir is auspicious, Ganadhar Gautam Swämi is auspicious; Ächärya Sthulibhadra is auspicious; Jain religion is auspicious.

मंगलं भगवान वीरो, मंगलं गौतमो गणि ।
मंगलं कुन्दकुन्दार्यो, जैन धर्मोस्तु मंगलं ॥

mangalam bhagaväna viro, mangalam gautamo gani I
mangalam kundakundäryo, jaina dharmostu mangalam II

Bhagawän Mahävir is auspicious, Ganadhar Gautam Swämi is auspicious; Ächärya Kunda-kunda is auspicious; Jain religion is auspicious.

अर्हन्तो भगवंत इन्द्रमहिताः, सिद्धाश्च सिद्धिस्थिता ।
आचार्या जिनशासनोन्नतिकराः, पूज्या उपाध्यायकाः ।
श्री सिद्धान्तसुपाठका मुनिवरा, रत्नत्रयाराधकाः ।
पंचै ते परमेष्ठिनः प्रतिदिनम्, कुर्वंतु वो मंगलम् ॥

arhanto bhagavanta indramahitäh, siddhäshcha siddhisthitä I
ächäryä jinashäsanonnatikaräh, püjyä upädhyäyakäh I
shri siddhäntasupäthakä munivarä, ratnatrayäradhakäh I
panchai te paramesthinah pratidinam kurvantu vo mangalam II

The Omniscients who have been worshipped by heavenly gods; the liberated souls, who are Siddhas; the heads of the religious order, who reinforce the fourfold order established by the Jinas; the revered Upädhyäys; well versed in the scriptures and the Saints who are also the followers of the true path of liberation (three jewels); may all these five auspicious entities bestow blessings on you everyday.

आदिमं पृथिवीनाथ-मादिमं निष्परिग्रहम् ।
आदिमं तीर्थनाथं च ऋषमस्वामिनं स्तुमः ॥

ädimam prthivinatha-mädimam nisparigraham I
ädimam tirthanätham cha rsabhasväminam stumah II

We adore Lord Rushabhadev who was the first king, who was the first to renounce all his possessions (everything) and who was the first Tirthankar.

तुभ्यं नमस्त्रिभुवनार्तिहराय नाथ, तुभ्यं नमः क्षीतितलामलभूषणाय ।
तुभ्यं नमस्त्रिजगतः परमेश्वराय, तुभ्यं नमो जिन भवोदधिशोषणाय ॥

tubhyam namastribhuvanärtiharäya nätha |
tubhyam namah ksititalämalabhüsanäya |
tubhyam namastrijagatah parameshvaräya |
tubhyam namo jina bhavodadhishosanäya ||

Lord, bow to you, the eradicator of misery of the three worlds; bow to you the adorable ornament on the face of the earth; bow to you, the Lord of the three worlds; omniscient Lord; bow to you, the destroyer of the sea of the life cycle.

वीरः सर्वसुरासुरेन्द्र-महितो, वीरं बुधाः संश्रिताः
वीरेणाभिहतः स्वकर्म निचयो, वीराय नित्यं नमः ।
वीरात् तीर्थमिदं प्रवृत्तमतुलं, वीरस्य घोरं तपो
वीरे श्री धृति कीर्ति कांति निचयः श्री वीर भद्रं दिश ॥

virah sarvasuräsurendra-mahito, viram budhäh samshritäh
virenäbhihatah svakarma nichayo, viräya nityam namah |
virat tirthamidam pravrttamatulam, virasya ghoram tapo
vire shri dhrti kirti känti nichayah shri vira ! bhadram disha ||

Lord Mahävir is worshipped by all heavenly gods as well as demons; the learned take refuge in Lord Mahävir; who has destroyed all his karma; I always bow to Lord Mahävir; this unparalleled Tirtha has been set up by Lord Mahävir; Lord Mahävir's austerities were intense; collections of enlightenment (Shri means wealth, here wealth of knowledge), patience, glory, and grace rest in Vir; Oh Lord Mahävir, show me the path to attain bliss.

उपसर्गाः क्षयं यान्ति, छिद्यन्ते विघ्नवल्लयः ।
मनः प्रसन्नतामेति, पूज्यमाने जिनेश्वरे ॥

upasargäh ksayam yänti, chhidyante vighnavallayah |
manah prasannatämeti, püjyamäne jineshvare ||

All the troubles disintegrate, the shackles of obstacles break, the mind achieves a blissful state wherever and whenever the Lord Jineshvars are worshipped.

शिवमस्तु सर्वजगतः, परहितनिरता भवन्तु भूतगणाः ।
दोषाः प्रयांतु नाशं, सर्वत्र सुखीभवतु लोकः ॥

shivamastu sarvajagatah, parahitaniratä bhavantu bhütaganäh |
dosäh prayäntu näsham, sarvatra sukhibhavatu lokah ||

May the entire universe attain bliss; may all beings be oriented to the interest of others; let all faults be eliminated; and may people be happy everywhere.

खामेमि सव्वजीवे, सव्वे जीवा खमन्तु मे ।
मित्ती मे सव्व भुएसु, वेरम् मज्झं न केणइ ॥

khämemi savvajive, savve jivä khamantu me |
mitti me savva bhuesu, veram majjham na kenai ||

I forgive all souls; let all souls forgive me. I am on friendly terms with all. I have no animosity towards anybody.

A

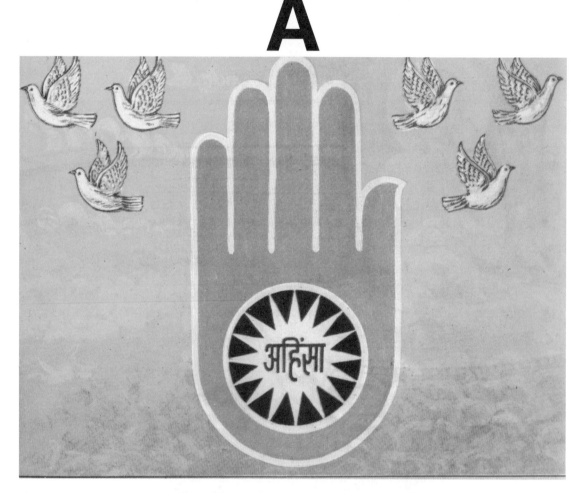

Ahimsä

A is for Ahimsä

Ahimsä means Non-Violence

More than 2500 years ago, Lord Mahävir made a simple yet powerful statement about Ahimsä;

"All life is just like me. I want to live. So do all living beings. Every living being wants to live and fears death. Each of us wants to be free from pain. So we should carry out all our activities with great care not to harm any living being."

"Ahimsä Parmo Dharma" means 'Non-Violence is the highest religion'. The philosophy of Non-Violence is a way of life. We must respect all life forms in order to practice total Non-Violence. A vegetarian diet is one simple way to practice Ahimsä. We should not eat, drink, or wear any product made by hurting, torturing or killing animals.

In the picture the raised hand tells us to stop and think before we start any activity, speak to other people, or even think about others. We can hurt someone or commit violence by any of these three actions - words, thoughts or actions. We should stop and think before doing anything. This way, we will be able to observe the principles of Ahimsä in its true sense. The wheel in the hand reminds us that if we do not watch all our actions, our soul* cannot be freed from the cycle of birth, life and death.

Ahimsä (non-violence), Anekäntaväd (non-one sidedness) and Aparigraha (non-possessiveness) are the three 'A's of Jainism. All Jains should apply these principles in their daily life.

* Soul is our true inner self; the part of us that never dies. See S

Note : A is also for Arihanta and Amity (friendship)

B

Bowing Down

B is for Bowing (Vandan)

Bowing is a method of Paying Respect

We bow to Tirthankars (Arihantas) and Siddha* Bhagawäns. We also bow down to Ächäryas**, Upädhyäys**, and all Sädhus and Sädhvis***. By bowing, we show our respect to them and admire their effort and spiritual achievements. We also bow to our parents, grandparents, and our teachers because we want to show our respect for them and thank them for what they have done for us. In this picture, a man is bowing. When we bow we become more humble.

So remember, respect others by bowing down.

Note : B is also for Bhakti, Bliss, and Bhagawän

Look for

*   Siddha under *N and S,

**   Ächäryas and Upädhyäys under N,

*** Sädhus and Sädhvis -under G

C

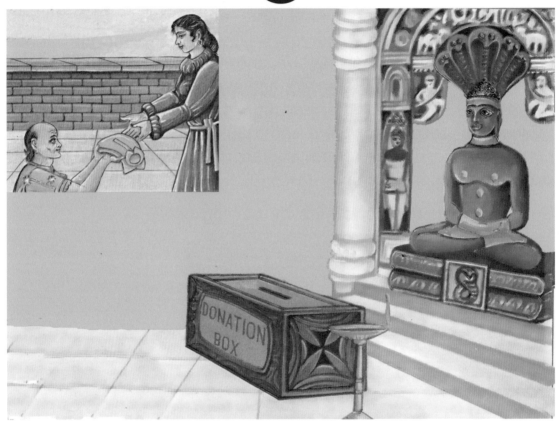

Charity

C is for Charity

Charity means to Share What We Have with Others

Charity is when we give something to others without expecting anything in return. Everyone, however big or small can give something to others. Charity is not just giving money, a person can share whatever they have as charity.

We should give food, clothing, medicine, and other articles of our own possession to needy people, give our time and skills to our community, and give respect and understanding to all living beings. The food offered should be vegetarian and offered with compassion.

Jains should always give anonymously (without the knowledge of others), free from pomp and ego. When we give in this manner, we get great satisfaction and happiness from within. The sole purpose of a donation box (Bhandär) in a temple is to encourage anonymous giving within each individual's capacity. Also in the picture, a girl is giving clothes to a needy person.

If we would have used our additional wealth for our comfort and pleasure we would have acquired more sins. Therefore, charity saves us from sins.

Note : C is also for Conduct

D

Discipline

D is for Discipline

Discipline means A State Of Order

Discipline is living our life in harmony with certain principles or guidelines. Just as the banks of the river help the water reach its destination by giving it guidance and direction, discipline brings order and structure to our lives and our activities, and helps us reach our goals.

Some examples of Discipline are:

1. Waking up and going to sleep at a certain time everyday.
2. Praying every morning, night, and before meals.
3. Bowing before our elders in respect for their age, experience, and wisdom.
4. Controlling our anger even when provoked.
5. Finishing our work on time, every time.
6. Listening to our parents since they know what is best for us and our family.

Note : D is also for Dharma, Devotion, Darshan, and Deva, which is synonymous with Bhagawän (Arihanta and Siddha)

E

Evening Prayer

E is for Evening Prayer and Pratikraman

Evening Prayer and Pratikraman Should Remind Us To Think About What We Did Today And What We Should Try To Do Better Tomorrow

Prayer can be said at any time. The most important prayer in Jainism is the Navakär Mantra*. We should say the Navakär Mantra at least seven times in the morning when we get up and seven times in the evening before going to bed. In the picture, a boy and a girl are saying their evening prayers.

Another practice all Jains, should follow is called Pratikraman. Here we introspect - look within ourselves, and take' a survey of our day. We take full responsibility for our actions and truly forgive those who have hurt us in any 'way. We repent and apologize for all our misdeeds of the day and promise ourselves to be more careful and not to repeat the same in the future.

Prayers and Pratikraman help uplift our soul; and we should always do these in the morning and in the evening.

Note : E is also for Enlightenment, Equanimity

Look for Navakär Mantra under N*

F

Forgiveness

F is for Forgiveness

Forgiveness means Pardoning Someone Who May Have Caused Us Some Harm

Forgiveness helps us remove our anger, hostility and resentment towards others. It energizes us and makes our world more beautiful than ever. Jainism teaches us that Ahimsä* (non-violence to other living beings) and forgiveness should be the main actions of our daily life.

In life we always come across people who have hurt us, intentionally or unintentionally. But no matter how badly they hurt us, we should always forgive them unconditionally. We should always think that our present suffering is due to our past karma. Hence we should stay calm, not get angry, and should not try to get even.

In the picture, Lord Mahävir** is forgiving Chandkaushik, the snake, even though he bit Mahävir. Bhagawän Mahävir showed the way of forgiveness. We, as his followers, should also forgive those who hurt us. Forgiving helps our soul while anger hurts our soul. We first forgive others and then seek their forgiveness for our faults.

Just as Ahimsä is a part of our daily life, forgiveness should also be a part of our daily action.

Note : F is also for Faith

Look for

*Ahimsä under A,

**Mahävir under M

G

Guru

JAIN ALPHABET BOOK

G is for Guru (Sädhu and Sädhvi)

Gurus are our Religious Leaders and Teachers

Jain monks (Sädhus) and nuns (Sädhvis) are our gurus. These gurus are people like us who have voluntarily given up their worldly attachments and have accepted the five great vows* as a code of conduct to purify their souls from karma.

Our Gurus observe total Ahimsä (non-violence). They tell the truth. They do not take anything not properly given to them. They observe celibacy and do not enjoy material happiness. They do not keep any possessions, which are not useful in their religious activity. They have also given up relationships and attachment to their family and friends.

The Gurus study scriptures, perform meditation, and live a pious life. They voluntarily suffer many hardships to get rid of their karma. The Sädhus do not touch or sit close to Sädhvis, ladies, or girls and Sädhvis do not touch or sit close to Sädhus, men, or boys. Both Sädhus and Sädhvis stay in a separate Upäshray. Except for the rainy season, they do not stay in one place for more than a few days at a time.

Shvetämbar Sädhus and Sädhvis wear white clothes. They keep a few clothes, a few bowls to collect food, a Rajoharan (soft broom to clean), and a Muhapatti (mouth cover to protect the small living organisms in the air). Digambar Sädhus do not wear any clothes, while the Sädhvis wear white clothes. Digambar Sädhus keep a Morpichhi (a broom made from naturally shredded peacock feathers) and a Kamandal (water utensil to wash).

Gurus from both traditions walk barefoot so that they do not hurt bugs or insects.

They do not keep money, jewelry, or own anything, such as a house or a car. They do not cook for themselves and do not eat any food that is cooked especially for them. They eat only vegetarian food.

The Jain Sangha (congregation) is made up of Sädhus, Sädhvis, Shrävaks (laymen) and Shrävikäs (laywomen). Many Jain Sanghas exist in various Jain sects. An Ächärya is the head of a Jain Sangha. They teach laypeople about religion. We respect gurus for their discipline and teachings. We take spiritual refuge in our gurus.

Note : G is also for God and Goodness

Look for *Vows under V

Parshwanäth Temple

Khajuraho Temples, Madhya Pradesh 9th Century

H

Help

H is for Help

Help means to Provide Service to the Needy

We should be helpful to everyone who needs our help and support. We should not forget anyone. Jainism says that we should help all people regardless of their caste, race, sex, and religion and whether they are good or bad people. We should help not only human beings, but also animals and other small living beings.

We can help in many different ways such as giving money, clothes, food, medicine, shelter, and education. We can also help by making a person feel better if they are sad. If someone requests something from us and we have only a little, we should share what we have. In the picture, the boys are helping a blind man to cross the road.

We must make it a habit to help others.

Note : H is also for Honesty

I

Indrabhuti Gautam

I is for Indrabhuti Gautam
Indrabhuti Gautam (also known as Gautam Swämi) was Bhagawän Mahävir's* First Disciple

Indrabhuti Gautam was the most well-known and educated Hindu Brahmin during the time of Lord Mahävir. He was a very knowledgeable person, and therefore became very arrogant. One day during a religious ceremony, he saw some celestial beings flying towards his town. He told everyone, "See, how great I am! Even heavenly angels have decided to join my religious ceremony." But the celestial beings did not stop to join him. Indrabhuti Gautam was surprised and inquired where the angels were going. The people said that the angels were going to pay their respect to Bhagawän Mahävir, who had come to the nearby Mahäsen forest. After attaining kevaljnän, Bhagawän Mahävir was to deliver his first sermon.

Immediately Indrabhuti visited Bhagawän Mahävir and saw his bright but humble personality. He experienced true happiness when he saw Bhagawän Mahävir. Bhagawän Mahävir explained to him the true meaning of the nature of the soul and its qualities. Indrabhuti was amazed and realized that Mahävir possessed kevaljnän (total knowledge) and had attained eternal happiness. His ego dissolved immediately and Indrabhuti bowed down to Bhagawän Mahävir and became his first disciple or Ganadhar. Later, he came to be known as Gautam Swämi.

For the next 30 years, Gautam Swämi asked many questions related to Jain philosophy and conduct to Bhagawän Mahävir. The answers to these questions are recorded in our Jain scriptures known as Ägam Sutras.

Gautam Swämi attained kevaljnän on the day after Bhagawän Mahävir attained nirvana. Bhagawän Mahävir's nirvana day was the last day (Deepävali day) of the Jain and Hindu calendar year and Gautam swämi's kevaljnän day was the first day (New Year day) of the Jain and Hindu calendar year. Hence, we begin our new year with a special prayer to Gautam Swämi and conclude the year with a special prayer to Bhagawän Mahävir.

We should give up our ego like Gautam Swämi.

Note : I is also for Image and Integrity

Look for *Mahävir under M

Ajitnäth Temple

Taranga Hills, Gujarat 11th Century

J

Jai Jinendra

J is for Jai-Jinendra

Jai-Jinendra means "Praise To The Jina."

"Jai Jinendra" helps us honor the virtues of our Tirthankar* or Jina. Jai Jinendra means, "May the religion established by the Jina prevail in our hearts". As we greet others we say, "Jai Jinendra" because we see the image of a Jina, conqueror of all inner enemies, in them. Recognizing this, we bow with respect to their Soul as every Soul is capable of becoming a Jina. When we see others in this light, we are more respectful and our behavior towards them changes. Our anger and ego dissolves immediately and we refrain from deceitful behavior.

Every morning when we awake and every night before we go to bed, we should respectfully say, "Jai Jinendra" to our parents, sisters, brothers, and grandparents. We should say, "Jai Jinendra" to any guests who visit our home. We should also say, "Jai Jinendra" to our teachers, other students at Jain Päthashälä**, and other Jains whom we may see at the Jain Center, Temple, Upäshray or any other place. We should greet our friends with "Jai Jinendra" when we talk on the telephone. In the picture, the boy is respectfully saying "Jai Jinendra" to his parents.

Remember; always greet others by saying "Jai Jinendra".

* Those who have established the Jain Religion order

Note : J is also for Justice and Jina

Look for **Pathshala under P

K

Karma

K is for Karma

Karma is the End Result of Our Action.

Every moment of our life, we are doing something either by words, thoughts or actions. We should remember that all activities - words, thoughts and actions collect karma. There are two kinds of karmas: good and bad. When we do good things, like helping or sharing with others, we collect good karmas. However, when we do something bad, like getting angry, screaming, or cheating, we collect bad karma.

Both good and bad karma produce results. If we get bad karma, then we will have to suffer in the future. Our life will be sad and miserable. However, if we get good karma, our life will be comfortable and happy. Whether one is rich or poor, strong or handicapped, a human or an animal, all are the result of our karma acquired in the past. Hence we should do good things that will make us happy in the future.

There are a total of eight types of karma that determine all aspects of our life and personality. Arihantas are born with eight types of karmas - they destroy four types of karmas when they attain omniscience and the other four when they attain nirvana and become a Siddha. Siddha Bhagawäns are pure soul, having no karma.

In the top picture, the man is shooting a bird and thus he will get bad karma. In the bottom picture, the girl is donating clothes to a needy person and thus she will get good karma. We should be careful of what we do and how we do it, because every moment we collect Karma.

Note : K is also for Knowledge

L

Leshyä

L is for Leshyä

Leshyä is the Thought Process Behind Any Action

In Jainism, there is a great deal of importance given to Leshyä. Leshyä refers to the state of mind. Our activities reflect our state of mind. The following illustration shows us how our activities vary with the state of our mind.

Once a group of six friends were traveling together. On the way, they got lost in the forest. They were hungry and thirsty, but they could not find anything to eat or drink. Then one of them noticed a fruit tree. They ran to it.

Each one had their own idea on how to obtain the fruits from the tree:

- The first friend wanted to chop down the whole tree.
- The second friend thought that they should just chop off the big branches.
- The third friend said that they only needed to chop off a few small branches, which held the fruits.
- The fourth one thought it unnecessary to chop any branches. They should just pick all the fruits from the tree.
- The fifth friend felt that they should pick enough fruits to satisfy their hunger. They should not waste any fruits.
- The sixth one said that there were enough fruits that had already fallen from the tree. They should not climb the tree, cut branches or pick fruits, when there were many good fruits on the ground.

See how differently the six friends thought? The first one wanted to destroy the whole tree while the sixth one did not want to hurt the tree at all. You can see how differently people can think. The way the sixth man thought was the best way and the way the first man thought was the worst way.

There are six Leshyäs, which describe the way people think in this story.

- First Leshyä is called the Black (Krishna) Leshyä (worst Leshyä)
- Second Leshyä is called the Blue (Neel) Leshyä
- Third Leshyä is called the Gray (Kapot) Leshyä
- Fourth Leshyä is called the Red (Tejo) Leshyä
- Fifth Leshyä is called the Yellow (Padma) Leshyä
- Sixth Leshyä is called the White (Shukla) Leshyä (best Leshyä)

Our thoughts change all the time and so will our Leshyä. We should always strive to think like the sixth man did. This will happen when we lessen our needs and wants, and when we think of others first instead of just ourselves.

Note : L is also for Liberation and Love

Kirti Sthambha

Chittorgarh, Rajasthan 12th Century

M

Mahävir

JAIN ALPHABET BOOK

M is for Mahävir

Mahävir is the 24th Tirthankar*

Lord Mahävir was born in 599 BC in Kshatriya-kund (also known as Kundalpur). His father was King Siddhärtha and his mother was Queen Trishalä**. Soon after it became known that queen Trishalä was pregnant, the people in King Siddhärtha's kingdom began noticing that business and farming were improving. King Siddhärtha believed that this was because Queen Trishalä was going give a birth to a very virtuous son. When the baby was born, they named him "Vardhamän" which means ever growing or increasing.

As he grew older, Prince Vardhamän showed himself to be a brave person. Once, while playing with his friends a snake came near them. Everyone was scared except Prince Vardhamän. He remained calm. He gently caught the snake, and put it in a safe place.

Another time, they were playing hide-and-seek. Whoever was caught would have to give a piggyback ride to the winner. A new boy joined the game. Soon, Prince Vardhamän caught him, and the boy gave the Prince a piggyback ride. Suddenly the new boy started to grow taller and scarier. The other boys became scared and ran away. Some of them climbed into a tree, and some ran to tell their parents.

While all this was going on, Prince Vardhamän was enjoying the ride. When he realized that the boy was not a real boy but he was a big monster, he gave the demon one blow between the shoulders with his fist. The monster could not take the pain and gave up his giant body. He told Prince Vardhamän that he is not a monster but an angel from heaven. He wanted to test his fearlessness and strength. He asked the Prince for forgiveness*** for his action and the Prince forgave him. The angel named Prince Vardhamän 'Mahävir', meaning "the strong one".

We should try to be brave and fearless like Lord Mahävir.

Note : M is also for Moksha

* A Tirthankar is one who re-establishes the religious order of monks, nuns, laymen and laywomen. This four-fold order is known as Jain Sangha

Look under

**Queen Trishalä under Q,

***Forgiveness under F

Indra Sabha (Courtyard)

Ellora Caves, Maharashtra 8th-10th Century

N

Namokär Mantra

N is for Namokär Mantra

The Namokär Mantra is the Most Important Prayer in Jainism

The sacred Jain prayer is the Namokär, Namaskär or Navakär Mantra in which homage is paid to the five worshipful personalities: Arihantas, Siddhas, Ächäryas, Upädhyäys, and all Sädhus and Sädhvis.

Namo Arihantänam
I bow to the Arihantas (Tirthankars) who have reached enlightenment by overcoming their inner weaknesses, who have attained infinite knowledge, vision, bliss, and power and have shown the path which brings an end to the cycle of life, death and suffering.

Namo Siddhänam
I bow to the Siddhas or liberated souls who have attained the state of perfection and immortality by liberating themselves from all karmas.

Namo Äyariyänam
I bow to the Ächäryas, who are the head of Jain congregations, and who preach the principles of religion and show the path of liberation, which is the unity of Right Faith, Right Knowledge, and Right Conduct.

Namo Uvajjhäyänam
I bow to the Upädhyäys who are the ascetic teachers. They explain Jain scriptures and show us the importance of the spiritual life over the material life.

Namo Loe Savva Sähunam
I bow to all the ascetics who strictly follow the five great vows of conduct and inspire us to live a simple life.

Eso Pancha Namukkäro
To these five types of great souls I offer my praise.

Savva Päva Ppanäsano
Such praise will help diminish my negative vibrations and sins.

Mangalänam cha Savvesim

Padhamam Havai Mangalam

Offering this praise is the most auspicious of all benedictions.

We should always recite the Namokär Mantra to pay respect to these great souls. This leads us to pure thoughts, which in turn leads to pure activities. We should recite it when we awake in the morning, going to bed at night or when we get free time.

Note : N is also for Non-attachment

Color Science of Navakär Mantra

Each line of the Navakär Mantra is associated with specific colors
and they have close connection with various Energy centers of the
body (please see the explanation at the end of this book).

O

Om

JAIN ALPHABET BOOK

O is for Om

Om is for meditation

Om is a holy word used in the beginning of many prayers. Om is also used to set a tune for meditation. Om is another religious chant like the Namokär Mantra**.

'Om' is a Sanskrut word and it sounds like 'Aum'. It is made up of five letters: - a, a, ä (aa), u, and m.

The five letters, spoken together, make the sound Om.

- The first letter "a" represents Arihanta (a human being who has realized the true nature of reality and has conquered their worldly passions)

- The second "a" represents Ashariri (Ashariri means to be without a physical body, such as a liberated soul, a perfected being, or a Siddha)

- The third letter "ä" represents Ächärya (an Ascetic who is the head of a Jain congregation)

- The fourth letter "u" represents Upädhyäy (an Ascetic teacher)

- The fifth letter "m" represents Muni (Sädhus and Sädhvis who practice Jain principles).

Hence, the Om represents the salutation to the five revered personalities in Jainism. Om is a short form of the Navakär or Namokär Mantra.

Note : O is also for Omniscience

Look for ** Navkär Mantra under N

P

Päthashälä

P is for Päthashälä

Päthashälä is a Place Where We Learn About Jainism.

A Päthashälä is a place where we can learn about our religion. Almost all Jain centers in North America have a Päthashälä. Many of the centers have Päthashälä classes on each Sunday.

Children should go to the Päthashälä so they can learn more about our religion. Parents should make sure that their children get a chance to go there.

So, remember to go to your Päthashälä to learn more about Jain Religion.

Note : P is also for Penance, Pujä, Pratikraman, and Prayer

Q

Queen Trishalä

JAIN ALPHABET BOOK

Q is for Queen Trishalä

Queen Trishalä Had Fourteen (Sixteen) Dreams After Lord Mahävir's* Soul Entered Her Womb

Queen Trishalä had fourteen dreams when she became pregnant. (According to Digambar tradition, Queen Trishalä had sixteen dreams adding a pair of fish and a lofty throne.) All the dreams symbolized the good qualities of her child. Queen Trishalä was very happy to be having such a wonderful child. That child was Lord Mahävir*. He showed us the path to freedom from the cycle of birth and death.

The fourteen (Shvetämbar tradition) / sixteen (Digambar tradition) dreams were:

01 Lion	02 Elephant
03 Bull	04 Goddess Lakshmi
05 Pair of Garlands	06 Full Moon
07 Sun	08 Flag
09 Golden Vase	10 Lotus Lake
11 Milky Ocean	12 Celestial Plane
13 Heap of Jewels	14 Smokeless Fire
15 Pair of Fish**	16 Throne**

Rushabhadev's mother dreamt of Bull, Elephant and Lion; while the mothers of Tirthankars number two to twenty-three dreamt of Elephant, Bull and Lion. The rest of the dreams were always in the same order.

Note : Q is also for Quest and Quality

Look for *Mahävir under M

** Additional dreams indicated in Digambar tradition

R

Rosary

R is for Rosary

Rosary is Used for Meditation*

Usually, we say the Namokär Mantra** in the morning and in the evening. Some people say it three to seven times, and some people say it 108 times. It would be hard to count 108 and meditate at the same time. To help us we use a rosary. A rosary has 108 beads and these beads represent the sum total of the 108 attributes of the five worshipful personalities (Pancha Parmeshtis):

Arihantas - 12

Siddhas - 08

Ächäryas - 36

Upädhyäys - 25

Sädhus - 27

This reminds us to aim for these 108 attributes ourselves.

To meditate on the Namokär Mantra we should sit in a quiet place, preferably facing east, everyday. We should forget everything else and concentrate on the 5 great souls in the Namokär Mantra. This will destroy our bad karma*** and bring good thoughts into our minds. It will give us peace.

Note : R is also for Respect, Reverence, and Reincarnation

* Meditation means to pray with spiritual thoughts

Look for **Namokär Mantra under N

***Karma under K

S

Soul (Ätmä)

S is for Soul (Ätmä)
Soul is immortal

Siddha Bhagawän is a pure soul, which is blissful and omniscient

All souls are immortal. All life forms have a soul and a body. Our body and our abilities are determined partly by the results of our karma*. When karma binds to our soul, the soul gets contaminated. Contaminated souls occupy four types of body forms: human, heavenly, hellish, or animals and plants (tiryancha) as depicted on the Swastika.

Even though the body and the soul are different, the body is the instrument through which we collect or remove Karma from our soul. Upon our death the soul and Karma migrate to a new body. The new body for the soul is determined by the Karma produced in our current lifetime. When all the attached karma are destroyed, the pure soul is permanently liberated from the body and attains liberation. This is also known as Nirväna. The pure soul reaches the top of the universe, called Moksha, and resides there forever. These souls are called Siddhas.

In the state of pure soul, as a Siddha, the soul does not go through the cycle of birth and death. In that state of being, the immortal soul is free, remains blissful for ever.

As Jains, Purification of our soul is our goal.

Note : S is also for Swastika, Sämäyika, Sädhu, and Sädhvi

Siddha** souls are venerable and we seek refuge in those.

Look for *Karma under K

T

Temple

T is for Temple

Temple Is A Place For Prayer And Worship

A temple is a place of worship where a person experiences immense peace and serenity. The images of Tirthankars and the temple's environment promote introspection and bring home the feeling that God resides within one's own heart. Therefore, each person can follow a path of purification of the inner self devoid of anger, greed, ego, deceit, and attachment from their lives.

The idols of Tirthankar Bhagawän are placed in Jain temples and we go there to worship them. When we enter the temple, we say Nissihi, meaning 'to refrain from', reminding us to leave behind our worldly thoughts and think only of our soul.

The purpose of worship is to pay respect to Tirthankars for their compassion and for showing us the true path for our liberation. This also reminds us that we should put all our efforts to become like them. Just praying and not taking any action to free our soul does not work. We must take action to discipline ourselves so that we can control our desires and passions and be compassionate towards others.

We should regularly visit the Temple. Some sects of Jainism do not worship idols in temple but they meditate in the Upäshray.

Note : T is also for Truth

U

Upäshray

U is for Upäshray

Upäshray is a Place Where Sädhus* or Sädhvis* Stay

The place where Sädhus and Sädhvis stay is called an Upäshray. An Upäshray is a very simple place with a big hall and a few small rooms that are kept cool by many windows. An Upäshray does not have any furniture except for a few wooden beds on which the Sädhus or Sädhvis sit and sleep. The Sädhus and the Sädhvis deliver their religious sermons in the Upäshray.

Sädhus or Sädhvis do not stay more than a few days at one Upäshray except during the rainy season. Sädhus and Sädhvis do not stay together in the same Upäshray at the same time.

An Upäshray is also a place where laypeople study religion, perform Sämäyika and Pratikraman, and celebrate religious ceremonies. It is a quiet place that one can spend time for introspection.

Note : U is also for Upädhyäy and Upayoga

Look for *Sädhu and Sädhvi under G

V

Vow

V is for Vow

Vow means a Promise

A vow is an earnest promise or pledge that binds one to a specified act or mode of behavior. To take a vow means we make a promise to ourselves to do certain things in certain ways or not to do certain things. Different vows can be for different lengths of time. A vow is a form of austerity (Tap) to help us discipline ourselves, reduce bad karma, and accumulate good karma. Some examples of external vows are as follows:

- Chauvihär - Not to eat and drink from sunset to sunrise
- Ekäsanu - To eat only one meal a day
- Upaväs - Not to eat for thirty-six hours starting from sunset the day before till sunrise the next day

Some examples of internal vows are as follows:

- Sämäyika - To sit peacefully in one place for forty eight minutes without being affected by worldly thoughts and activities brings peace and reduces stress in our life.
- Mauna - Not to speak for a certain time (Speech can be a large source of violence)
- Donating anonymously can be an important vow to control our ego.
- Setting limits to our needs can be an important vow to control our greed.

Internal vows are harder to keep but they benefit us the most. The vows we take should be observed very carefully.

Note : V is also for Victory, Vision, and Virtues

W

Worship

JAIN ALPHABET BOOK

W is for Worship

Worship means to Pray

The respectful love shown to an idol, deity or sacred object is called worship. Prayers and ceremonies express this love. Jains show their ardent devotion to Arihanta (Tirthankar or Jina) and Siddha Bhagawäns* who have freed themselves from the cycle of birth and death.

We worship them to remind ourselves that they are liberated souls and that we want to be like them. Worshiping also helps to uplift our soul and realize that it can be free from attachment and aversion. We can also be liberated through the practice of the principles of Jainism: Non-violence (Ahimsä), Truth (Satya), Non-stealing (Achaurya), Celibacy (Brahmacharya) and Non-possessiveness (Aparigraha).

Worshiping is done through prayers, ceremonies and meditation. Worshiping can be done in a temple, an Upäshray, at a Jain center, or even at home.

We should worship with our heart and mind and not just for show.

Note : W is also for Wisdom

Look for *Siddha under S

X

Xylography

JAIN ALPHABET BOOK

X is for Xylography

Xylography is the Art of Carving Wood

Xylography is the art of carving wood. This art has been a specialty in the state of Gujarat and Karnataka in India.

There are woodcarvings of Jina idols, deities, and auspicious symbols in the window frames, domes, and arches of Jain houses. There are some temples with exquisite woodcarvings made in the fourteenth century. The circular carvings in this picture represent the endless world. The Tirthankars remind us to move beyond this cycle of birth and death and thus be free from miseries.

Xylography art is seen in many Jain temples.

Y

Yoga

Y is for Yoga

Yoga means Activities

In Jainism all our physical, verbal, and mental activities are known as Yoga (Yog). All these activities, good or bad, collect karma* and get attached to our soul. Therefore, we should control our activities. We can do this by paying attention to what we do, say and think. It is easy to control physical activities, but it is harder to control our speech. Mental activities are the most difficult to control. We should be careful when we want to do something, and be sure that we are not doing, saying or thinking anything that could be hurtful to others or to ourselves.

According to Jain religion, yoga and meditation are two different things. Yoga means our activities and meditation means focusing the mind on specific thoughts.

The similar word yogä has been accepted in English to mean light physical exercise. Many people perform physical yogä, which helps control verbal and mental activities.

Look for *Karma under K

Z

Zälar

Z is for Zälar

Zälar is a Musical Instrument

A Zälar is played in some of the rituals performed in the temple. It is made of brass and it looks like a thick disk. It is played with the help of a wooden hammer that is tapped on the metal disk to make varying sounds. It is generally used at religious activities in front of an idol.

Color Science of Navakär Mantra

Namo Arihantänam - White Color:

Arihanta is a perfect human being. White color represents Arihanta. White color is the mother of all colors; it is a blending of all colors. It represents pure knowledge. White light removes the diseases from the body, mind, and soul. White blood cells protect the body from disease and control its energy. White color shows purity, selflessness, and cosmic consciousness. White has protective power against psychic attack. This power should not be used for personal gain.

Namo Siddhänam - Red Color:

Siddha is a pure consciousness or a soul without any Karma attached to it. Both Arihanta and Siddha are known as Gods in Jainism. Red color represents Siddha. Red color is the great energizer. Red controls the energy center of command. This center governs the vitality of the physical body, particularly the creative, procreative, and restorative process.

Namo Äyariyänam - Yellow and Orange Color:

Ächärya is a head of a Jain congregation. It symbolizes the self-control, discipline and organizational power. Yellow or orange color represents Ächärya. Both yellow and orange colors represent wisdom, power to accomplish goals, and strong will power (discipline) in life.

Yellow stimulates the Solar Plexus and controls the digestive processes in the stomach. It strengthens the nervous system and awakens reasoning facilities. It controls eliminative action of the intestines and liver.

Orange assists in assimilation, distribution, and circulation of body functions. It acts mentally on assimilation of new ideas, relieves repression, and combines physical energy and wisdom.

Namo Uvajjhäyanäm - Dark Green and Blue Color:

Upädhyäy is a teacher, who shows how to awaken powers and maintain the balance of body, mind, and soul. Green or Blue color represents Upädhyäy.

Green is the color of balanced strength and of progress in the mind and body. It controls the energy center of the heart. It has a soothing influence on the nervous system. It is tonic for the body, mind, and soul.

Blue is the color of truth. It gives power of speech. It is relaxing, soothing, and healing. Blue rays bring calmness and peace to the mind. It is the color of religious aspiration and devotion. Blue rays can transmit thought energy. Blue effects the development of spiritual and psychic powers. Both blue and green are also the colors of vital energy (präna).

While yellow is the color of wisdom (mind), and blue is the color of truth (soul), green is the combination of the two, offering a balance between the two.

Namo Loe Savva Sähunam - Black Color:

Both Sädhu (monk) and Sädhvi (nun) are spiritual practitioners. The practitioner must be protected from worldly attachments and must destroy negativity. Black color represents the practitioner. Black is the absence of all color. It is receptive, consumes negativity, and gives the strength to fight negativity. It controls the sensual energy center of the body.

Notes